Read by the poet
at the fiftieth anniversary
of the founding of the United Nations
San Francisco
26 June 1995

A BRAVE AND STARTLING TRUTH

MAYA ANGELOU

A
BRAVE
AND
STARTLING
TRUTH

RANDOM HOUSE NEW YORK

Library of Congress Cataloging-in-Publication Data
is available.

ISBN 0-679-44904-3

Manufactured in the United States of America on acid-free paper

24689753

FIRST EDITION

This book is dedicated
to the hope for peace,
which lies, sometimes hidden,
in every heart.

A BRAVE AND STARTLING TRUTH

We, this people, on a small and lonely planet
Traveling through casual space
Past aloof stars, across the way of indifferent suns
To a destination where all signs tell us
It is possible and imperative that we learn
A brave and startling truth.

And when we come to it
To the day of peacemaking
When we release our fingers
From fists of hostility
And allow the pure air to cool our palms

When we come to it

When the curtain falls on the minstrel show of
     hate

And faces sooted with scorn are scrubbed clean

When battlefields and coliseum

No longer rake our unique and particular sons and
     daughters

Up with the bruised and bloody grass

To lie in identical plots in foreign soil

When the rapacious storming of the churches
The screaming racket in the temples have ceased
When the pennants are waving gaily
When the banners of the world tremble
Stoutly in the good, clean breeze

When we come to it

When we let the rifles fall from our shoulders

And children dress their dolls in flags of truce

When land mines of death have been removed

And the aged can walk into evenings of peace

When religious ritual is not perfumed

By the incense of burning flesh

And childhood dreams are not kicked awake

By nightmares of abuse

When we come to it

Then we will confess that not the Pyramids

With their stones set in mysterious perfection

Nor the Gardens of Babylon

Hanging as eternal beauty

In our collective memory

Not the Grand Canyon

Kindled into delicious color

By Western sunsets

Nor the Danube, flowing its blue soul into Europe

Not the sacred peak of Mount Fuji

Stretching to the Rising Sun

Neither Father Amazon nor Mother Mississippi
who, without favor,

Nurture all creatures in the depths and on the
shores

These are not the only wonders of the world

When we come to it

We, this people, on this minuscule and kithless
    globe

Who reach daily for the bomb, the blade and the
    dagger

Yet who petition in the dark for tokens of peace

We, this people, on this mote of matter

In whose mouths abide cankerous words

Which challenge our very existence

Yet out of those same mouths

Come songs of such exquisite sweetness

That the heart falters in its labor

And the body is quieted into awe

We, this people, on this small and drifting planet
Whose hands can strike with such abandon
That, in a twinkling, life is sapped from the living
Yet those same hands can touch with such healing,
    irresistible tenderness,
That the haughty neck is happy to bow
And the proud back is glad to bend
Out of such chaos, of such contradiction
We learn that we are neither devils nor divines

When we come to it
We, this people, on this wayward, floating body
Created on this earth, of this earth
Have the power to fashion for this earth
A climate where every man and every woman
Can live freely without sanctimonious piety
Without crippling fear

When we come to it

We must confess that we are the possible

We are the miraculous, the true wonder of this
world

That is when, and only when

We come to it.